# The Secr Maı Didn't Tell You About Men™

"The MANual To Amazing Sex"

**Cv Pillay**

*The CEO Transformational SuccSex Coach*

To

JESSICA

HERE IS TO LEARNING
HOW TO HAVE AMAZING
SEX!! mmı

02/11/14

# The Secrets Your Mama Didn't Tell You About Men™
### "The MANual To Amazing Sex"

Cv Pillay

ISBN 978-0-9929282-0-9

Printed in the United Kingdom

This book is available online, in my training programs and in all amazing bookstores.

Cover By: Dagmara Rosiak (www.digirigi.com)

# *Foreword*

You might ask yourself why I should I buy this book over not any other sex books out there. With a great title like "The Secrets Your Mama Didn't Tell You About Men" you now have the answers to most of the questions all women normally have and nobody can or likes to answer.

With this book you have the solutions without having to try and find them out for yourself. There are many sex books out there but nothing like this as it makes you do exercises after every chapter of the book.

Cv Pillay has made a sex self-help book that will add more spice to your life in more ways than you can ever think of. I know you are going to love this book.

This book is not only on how *"To Get The Guy"*, but on having the guy stay because he wants to stay with you.

- Raymond Aaron, New York Times Best-Selling Author
*Double Your Income Doing What You Love*

# *Disclaimer - Please Read This*

Although anyone may find the practices, disciplines, games and understanding in this book to be useful, it is sold with the understanding that neither the author nor the publisher are engaged in presenting specific medical, psychological, emotional, sexual, or spiritual advice. Nor is anything in this book intended to be a diagnosis, prescription, recommendation or cure for any specific kind of medical, psychological, emotional, sexual or spiritual problem. Each person has unique needs and this book cannot take these individual differences into account. Each person should engage in a program of treatment, prevention, cure or general health only in consultation with a licensed, qualified physician, therapist, or other competent professional. Any person suffering from venereal disease or any local illness of his or her sexual organs or prostate gland should consult a medical doctor before practicing any sexual games described in this book.

---

## Power Quote

### *You Can't Change Your Past But...*
### *You Can Change Your Future.*

---

## *About The Author*

Cv Pillay is

"The CEO Transformational SuccSex Coach"

who specializes in helping you awaken your inner sexual

energy, while harnessing this newfound power to

passionately manifest your biggest visions and create the

life that you really want.

He has worked with Multi-Millionaires, CEOs,

Celebrity Actresses, Authors, Musicians, Coaches,

Trainers and Business Professionals. He regularly speaks

to and communicates with an audience that spans six

continents.

---

## Power Quote

*Our Paths Crossing, Was No Mistake.*

---

# *Acknowledgements*

## To My Mama

Thank you for all your love and guidance you gave me, for
the constant encouragement to always follow my
dreams and to never ever give up.
I Love You.

## To My Mentors And Coaches
(Influences From 1999 And Beyond)

Anthony "Tony" Robbins,
Richard Bandler,
Raymond Aaron, T. Harv Eker,
Blair Singer, John Gray,
Wayne Dyer, Oprah Winfrey,
Deepak Chopra, Paulo Coelho
Milton Erickson, Napoleon Hill,
Dale Carnegie,
Mahatma Gandhi and Nelson Mandela.

You are inspirational leaders at a time of great
change in this world.
I am grateful for all I have learned from you all.

## *Tips On How To Read This Book*

In today's fast-paced world the need to disseminate information and determine what is important to us is critical. This book has been written in an easy-to-read format and to convey maximum benefit in the shortest amount of time, while enabling *you* the reader to apply its benefits immediately.

There are of course different types of readers. There are the "nibblers" who like to read a little bit, come back later and read a little more. There are the moderate readers who take their time, as well as the voracious ones who will read the entire book in one sitting. You also have the "midnight snackers" who like to re-read little titbits to get re-focused and re-energized. My Power Quotes found throughout this book are perfect for everyone, especially the "midnight snackers".

There is no wrong way to read this book. I believe so strongly that these thoughts and ideas can help improve your sex life, the only way this book won't help you is if you don't finish this book!

PS. When you see the words *"Take Notes."*

Take Notes!!

You will see a change in your thinking. You may want to ask a friend to work with you when reading this book and the changes will happen much faster.

Also share notes with them to get more out.

Read this book with an open mind.

My book is made for you to read and practice,

to give you what you desire,

"Amazing Sex"

---

## Power Quote

*Not Finishing What You Start*

*Is Like Opening A Condom And Not Using It.*

---

# CONTENT

# BASIC ASSUMPTION OF THIS BOOK

Every book or author has a point of view, a set of basic assumptions underlining the principles and practices the author writes about. We all bring our personal history, education and experiences to the table when we speak or write.

Where is the origin to having "Amazing Sex"?

It's YOU!

You have learnt it from everybody around you.

You have at one stage of your life heard it, seen it, felt it, sensed it, or most times tasted it (You know want I mean).

Hence I can say, "Not everything in this book is new to you". Some of the games I have made are new!!… and you are going to love them!!

The first and foremost assumption in this book is that your life is a precious gift that you have been entrusted with from birth. You are given a body, a mind and a set of resources and limitations to work with. It is up to you to use what you have to make the most of what you have been given. The purpose of life is self-realization. To realize your true nature and potential.

Now you may be thinking what does that have to do with this book?

Sex is a vital aspect of your life or maybe the most important part of your life

"If your parents did not have sex that time"

(You know what I mean), you would not be reading this book now. You get my point and I must stress that this is the case for almost everybody. Now you are thinking about your parents having sex?

Okay you can…

## STOP NOW!!

Sex is also an amazing source of pleasure, joy, and fun. The experiences of a lifetime are the curriculum that allows you to learn about your true self and develop your natural gifts and talents.

If your life is like a school, The Sex and Intimate Relationships Class must not be an advanced class. If you welcome this book as an opportunity to learn about yourself and expand your capacity to deal creatively with your MAN, then you will feel and be happy almost all the time.

If by the time you have finished reading the first four chapters of this book and if you aren't then a little better equipped to meet your sex situations, then I shall consider this book to be a total failure, so far as you are concerned. For "The great aim of education", said Herbert Spencer, "Is not knowledge but action" and this is an action book.

---

## Power Quote

**_Without Action, Victory Bears No Fruit._**

---

# Quiz About You

Select the answers you identify with the most.

Answer them and pick the first one that comes to mind.

You will learn a lot from this simple quiz.

Use a pen or pencil and ring your answers:

1. How do others rate you as a lover?

   a) I have to beat them away with a stick

   b) Rather well, I hope

   c) No one has complained yet

   d) Who cares?

2. Is it important to give your MAN an orgasm?

   a) My partner always reaches an orgasm

   b) Very

   c) Not the most important thing

   d) Why? Doesn't everyone have orgasms?

3. What surfaces do you like to make love on?

   a) My partner's body

b) A mattress

c) Soft green grass

d) Anywhere, as long as we have fun

4. What's the most important thing for amazing sex?

a) Physical stamina

b) Imagination

c) The perfect body

d) An intelligent mind

5. Would you stop taking the quiz and make love now?

a) Yes

b) Is this a trick question?

c) Not until I see my score

d) Only if you promise it'll be worth it

---

## Power Quote

*Your Sex Life Is All About Choices And
What You Value Most.*

---

# *Scoring*

(1) a = 2,  b = 4,  c = 3,  d = 1

(2) a = 3,  b = 4,  c = 2,  d = 1

(3) a = 3,  b = 4,  c = 2,  d = 1

(4) a = 2,  b = 4,  c = 1,  d = 3

(5) a = 4,  b = 3,  c = 2,  d = 1

16–20. If you're at this end of the scale, you're a wild sex machine. You spend a lot of time thinking of and having sex. You relate well to the needs of your MAN.

11–15. You're not up there with the great ones, but at least you try. Work on the idea that you have to give as good as you get.

6–10. Do yourself and your MAN a favor and work through this book several times until you get it right.

0–5. Celibacy: Look it up in the dictionary and practice it for the rest of your life.

"The MANual To Amazing Sex"

# BENEFITS OF AMAZING SEX WITH YOUR MAN

1. This is very cost-effective relationship therapy. Practicing the understanding and communication techniques included in this book will greatly enhance your relationship skills.

2. Gives you emotional health. Happiness and satisfaction with life comes with having an amazing sexual connection.

3. Your MAN will greatly appreciate your bliss in the relationship.

4. Long, sexy, creative, affordable dates. You and your MAN will learn to cherish the time together and make every second count with a great big smile.

5. Knowledge, advice, and ideas to share with your girlfriends. You can pass or share tips to your friends to help them improve their relationships as well.

6. Gives you mental health. Amazing sex contributes to a better sense of personal growth, strengthens the connection

you have with your MAN, and will have a calming effect in your life.

7. Knowing that you are an amazing lover will make you glow.

8. You'll have so much more understanding of your MAN.

9. You will have more engagements to do together.

*Add Your Amazing Sex Benefits:*

_____

_____

_____

_____

_____

_____

---

## Power Quote

*No Sex With Your MAN Is Like A Car Without Any Wheels. You Both Won't Go Anywhere.*

---

# MISTAKES YOU MAY BE MAKING WITH YOUR MAN

## When You Act Like His Mother And Treat Your MAN Like Your Child

Firstly, I want you to think about this. Have you ever had a MAN, and when he got sick you treated him like a baby? Scolded him for not answering his mobile phone? Assuming he was forgetful and reminding him of stuff he needed to remember himself? This makes him feel like a child and you acting like his mother. The worst one is taking charge of activities that you assume he can't do right. If you are doing this, what happens? Your MAN has the feeling of his mother and then basically acts like your child.

And this is a funny topic. Have you ever said something like this?

"I called you all day and you didn't answer? Where were

you?"

"Where do you think you are going mister without a jacket? Don't you know it's cold outside?"

"Don't forget to call me when you are at the shop so I can remind you what to buy."

He is painting a wall and you say, " That is not how you paint a wall!" and grab the brush to show him.

There are many more examples of you acting like his "Mother ". The best way to figure out if you are doing the "Mother Act" is when you are telling him

"You need to act more like a MAN".

Just that line, or thinking this now, then you know you are doing this. Are you doing this?

*Take Notes.*

_____

_____

_____

_____

_____

_____

_____

_____

_____

_____

---

## Power Quote

*Never Look Down On Your MAN Unless*

*He Is In Between Your Legs.*

---

## When You Fall In Love With Your MAN's Future Potential

When Adam and Eve first met, Adam thought Eve was the most beautiful girl he had ever laid his eyes on.

But when Eve laid eyes on Adam what she saw was really amazing.

She saw a lifetime partner, a house, a dog named Snoopy, two kids and living in Beverly Hills. I am not saying you do this, but do think about it?

---

**Power Quote**

*If Life Was Like A Race:*

*If You Tell Me How To Run My Life,*

*One Day I May Run Out Of Yours.*

---

Here are some signs if you are doing this:

"He just needs a little more time to get his life together"

And you say this every few months.

"If I show him that I love him the most, he will change for me!"

"No one can see the real person inside him only I can"

Now like before we all have our own patterns.

To break this pattern might be quite hard!

"Is that what you are thinking now?"

The minute you plant this thought, "It will take a long time or I can't do it" this becomes a reality.

I know what you want because I can read your mind and I can see you smiling while you are reading this. While you are reading this now you are thinking "what's next?", or "how can I overcome or solve this?"

Guess what? The answer is in your mind because you created it in the beginning.

Here is "The Mind Fuck" If you want a fairy tale life, you will have to share this fairy tale story with the one you love.

If this MAN gets too scared when you are sharing this, then you will need to ask yourself one of two questions, "Is he the one for me?" or "Am I the one for him?"

*Take Notes.*

_____

_____

_____

_____

_____

_____

_____

_____

_____

_____

## **Not Initiating Sex With Your MAN**

Lots of my clients, and most of the women that I know, always tell me they worry about their ladylike behaviour when it comes to sex. "Sure", I tell them, "we men make our fair share of bedroom errors and I have made a lot." But as the saying goes, "it takes two to tango". As it turns out, top sex and relationship experts say that women make plenty of sex mistakes of their own. I know you don't want to appear pushy or come on too strong for fear of being labelled aggressive or a slut.

## Power Quote

### *The First Mistake You Make, Is Not Admitting That You Make Mistakes.*

As you read along with this book, you will see that most men actually fantasize and want to see the woman take charge in the bedroom when it comes to sex.

Show your interest by taking the first step from time to time. Your MAN will most likely appreciate it and you may find a new level of satisfaction in taking responsibility for your own sexual experiences.

This is something I feel strongly women must do.

What are you thinking now?

*Take Notes.*

_____

_____

_____

_____

_____

_____

_____

_____

_____

_____

## Worrying About What You Look Like

Thinking about how you look during sex stops you from enjoying yourself and ruins your chances of getting an orgasm, two, three or more.

Stop thinking about the fat on your tummy or the size of your boobs and start concentrating on the pleasure of the act. You must give yourself permission to have an orgasm.

Your MAN wants you to release yourself when it comes to sex play and go with the flow and that's not likely if you are anxious about your physical concerns. Most of the time your MAN doesn't notice half the things you obsess about anyway. *Sounds really bad but it is true.*

Your MAN will be more attracted to you when you show signs of health, youth and fertility. Rather than thinking about the shape of your waist and hips start thinking about your sexual energy, enthusiasm and how you want to connect with him more.

---

## Power Quote

*Your Biggest Mistake Is Giving Another Woman The Opportunity To Have Amazing Sex With Your MAN.*

---

Do you do this? Did anything come up in your mind?

*Take Notes.*

_____

_____

_____

_____

_____

_____

_____

_____

_____

_____

## <u>Thinking Your MAN Is Always Up For Sex</u>

STOP! I know you're thinking "Yeah Right", and you would be right if you were dating or married to most teenage boys because they are ready and willing just about any time you ask, but this is not always true for your MAN.  It comes from the pressures of everyday life - family, work, bills and money - Yes this can zap your MAN's libido and normally does. This does come as a big surprise to many of my clients. Often the lack of your

MAN's sex drive is most of the time taken personally by yourself.

One client told me "If he is not doing me then he is doing someone else". She had a shock and did not want to believe that he just was not in the mood for sex.

You know yourself that you are not always interested in sex but you still love your MAN. But when you discover he doesn't want to have sex, you think, "Wow, he doesn't love me anymore."

Not true. He just doesn't want to have sex now.

Are *you* doing this?

*Take Notes.*

_____

_____

_____

_____

_____

_____

_____

---

---

---

> # Power Quote
> *Change Your Thinking And This Will...*
> *Change Your Sexual Energy.*

## Getting Angry When He Suggests Something New In The Bedroom

I know this to be a 100% fact for me.

After being together for a good few years with my ex, one would think it's natural to want to spice things up with a little variety. Just because your MAN wants to try something new doesn't mean he's unhappy with you or the sex life. In short: *Don't Take It Personally.*

Still, it's good and important that you grow out of your comfort zone. No one is asking you to feel obligated to do something you don't want to do sexually.

---

## Power Quote

*Sex Is One Of Time And Nature's Masterpiece.*

---

If your MAN asks you to try something that's outside of your morals, make it clear that it's off limits for you and explain why. Of course, do this in a loving way as best as you can. If it's something that is not really a moral issue for you but you still don't want to, maybe it's a personal thing, again explain why.

If it's simply a startling request such as "Darling, I've just made a sex dungeon in the spare room, I'm want to tie you up"

If you're initially uneasy about it, try not to over react. Instead, just let him know you need some time to think about it.

*Take Notes.*

_____

_____

_____

_____

_____

_____

_____

_____

_____

## Not Giving Your MAN Guidance

Talking very directly about sex, what you like and don't like can make you feel uncomfortable, even with your MAN that you've been with for a long time and otherwise feel close to. But this is the only way to achieve an amazing sexual relationship.

You must take responsibility for your sexual encounters. Your MAN can't bring you to orgasm if you don't take responsibility for your sexual experiences. Even the best lovers can't know what you need without you letting them know.

---

## Power Quote

### *Your MAN Very Much Wants To Please You!*

---

If you can tell him in a way that doesn't kill his ego, he will appreciate it. Try to sandwich what you don't like in between four things you do when you are talking to him. You won't find out until the next time you're in bed with him. But we do listen, particularly if you're quite clear about it! Any ideas come to you?

*Take Notes.*

_____

_____

_____

_____

_____

_____

_____

_____

_____

_____

*A client once asked me:*

*"Cv, how do I get Mr Right?"*

*And my reply to her was:*

*"If you want to get Mr Right, you*

*must first become Mrs Right."*

### Have Any Questions For Me:
Feel free to call.

*My mobile number is: +(44) 778899 5678*

---

## Power Quote

**Treat Me Right And You Will See The Light,**

**Treat Me Wrong And You Will Be Gone.**

---

# Write Four Things
# That Are Sexy About You!

1. _____
   _____
   _____

2. _____
   _____
   _____

3. _____
   _____
   _____

4. _____
   _____
   _____

---

## Power Quote

### *The Worst Prison Would Be A Closed Mind.*

---

# Feedback To Yourself

1. What was my biggest insight whilst I was reading this chapter?

_____

_____

_____

_____

2. What action will I take now after reading this chapter?

_____

_____

_____

3. What support do I need to take this action?

_____

_____

_____

_____

# QUIZ ABOUT YOUR MAN

This quiz can be a real eye-opener. You learn by knowing how you feel or understand about your MAN.

Use a pen or pencil and ring your answers:

1. Will your MAN still be exciting at sixty-one?

   a) I hope to find out

   b) I can't imagine sleeping with a wrinkly

   c) Couples don't have sex then, do they?

   d) We'll keep the fire burning

2. Can you talk to your MAN about anything?

   a) Yes—and it doesn't always have to make  sense

   b) No—some subjects are taboo

   c) At the right time

   d) Always

3. Does your MAN lick you in all the right places?

   a) I am lucky to get kisses

   b) You would pay big money for my lover's tongue

c) When I ask

d) It's usually, "I'll lick yours, if you lick mine."

4. Does your MAN ever try new sexual things?

a) Yes—it helps keep the spice in our sex

b) Yes—I wonder where the ideas come from

c) We both introduce new things

d) No—It's always the same

5. Does your MAN still turn you on after all this time?

a) The flame is starting to flicker

b) In a stronger, more mature way

c) The physical attraction has become mental

d) Not in the mornings

6. Does your MAN show you affection in public?

a) It comes naturally

b) We only hold hands

c) Our relationship doesn't work like that

d) At the start of our relationship, but not now

# *Scoring*

(1) a = 3,  b = 2,  c = 1,  d = 4

(2) a = 4,  b = 1,  c = 2,  d = 3

(3) a = 1,  b = 4,  c = 3,  d = 2

(4) a = 3,  b = 2,  c = 4,  d = 1

(5) a = 1,  b = 4,  c = 3,  d = 2

(6) a = 4,  b = 3,  c = 2,  d = 1

19–24. Wow! Your MAN is every women's fantasy.

13–18. Sex and romance are working well. Don't let things slip and you'll reap the rewards forever.

7–12. Sounds like your MAN is a few condoms short of a full pack. Don't give up on him, use the suggestions in the book and you never know what might cum out.

0–6. Pack and leave now. With close to 7 billion people in this world you both deserve better.

# GAMES YOUR MAN WOULD LOVE TO PLAY

---

## Safer Sex Message

*Sexually active adults need to take responsibility for their own sexual health and wellbeing. This means being informed about safer sex methods and using them. As the author of this book, I cannot be held responsible for ensuring that when you try any sex techniques in this book that you do so safely.*

---

Playing games with your MAN will not only keep your MAN happy but will also ensure that he will not want to leave you. If he's having steak at home why will he go elsewhere for burgers? That's the metaphor I use with my clients to describe feelings or emotions they have, because food does play a vital role.

Women often say (and don't quote me on this), "Men have no feelings". But actually we do, we feel

hungry all the time… So we do feel!
I have cum up with some games to make you think
differently and many will take you out of
your comfort zone.

---

## Power Quote

*Nobody Makes Us Angry, We Decide*

*To Use Anger As A Response.*

---

## Angry Love

I wish I'd had this when I was married to my ex-wife,
because it would have given me a chance to express myself
more. There are some people like me who like to keep the
urge to breakout or explode until it is the last resort or as in
the Arabic proverb "The straw that broke the camel's
back". But if you are given the opportunity to talk every
week then you will have nothing to nag about, to be angry
about, or to complain about with your MAN, and after a

few weeks you may just start complimenting him.

You are thinking, "where is the fun in this game?" I wanted to make it fun and that is what I did as the creator of the game.

To play this game you will need a few props and there is one main rule you have to follow. Lets start off with the props. A stopwatch; most smart phones have them, a coin, and a pair of dice. Flip the coin to decide who goes first. Throw the dice to find out how many minutes your turn will last, this will be between two and twelve minutes. The main rule is that after the first week of playing, you can only talk about the last seven days. *The rest is history.* I've used this with most of my clients and they have had some amazing outcomes.

I am getting this game made as an app, while writing this book, and it may be out before or after the book is launched. No promises in the meantime.

Now, the purpose of this game is to let go of your feelings and the result may vary from person to person. If you are a fire starter and like having arguments, this will tone down your behaviour. If you are the total opposite and feel that you are not heard in the relationship, then this is your perfect time to be heard and tell your MAN exactly how you feel. Whether you like it or not women and men will always nag and argue, but if you had a timescale to do this, wouldn't it be okay and will make it a bit fun.

*Take Notes.*

_____

_____

_____

_____

_____

## **Truth or Dare?**

If you've never played this sex game you're in for a surprise. Whether you pick truth or dare, you're sure to uncover a few new and titillating things about your MAN and vice versa. All you need to play this game is a vivid imagination and a healthy sexual appetite. If you get stuck don't only ask about sexual fantasies, bring them to life. As for dare, a striptease or lap dance will always spice things up just a little bit more. From the get-go I would say have some rules, and if you don't want to talk about your ex-partners then please say so at the beginning. We don't want him getting jealous or something now do we? Or even you for that matter. This game can be used if you have a long-term partner and you just want to spice up the relationship, like how you do "Date Night" just call it "Sex Night".

---

## Power Quote

### *If You Want Something New, You Got To Do Something New.*

---

What I would recommend is start off by doing it once a month to see how comfortable you are with this.

If there is a flow then do it more. Don't *you* like to be teased or excited?

*Take Notes.*

_____

_____

_____

_____

_____

## **Making Time For Sex**

Yes you have your job, studies, kids, parents, friends, the dog, house cleaning and holidays... With so many things to juggle in life, finding the time for sex can be tricky. If you wait to initiate sex when you are in bed with your MAN you probably stand a greater chance of being rejected. Why you ask? It's simple. Your MAN's in bed because he is tired.

You can try initiating sex in the morning, but then you have the risk of needing to rush off to work instead, or you are just not a morning person. If your MAN enjoys a good night's sleep and you're a monster in the morning, think about when you both have the most free time and take full advantage of it. You can try weekends, after work (yes, before dinner), or long before bedtime. You can also be spontaneous and take a long lunch together or play hookey from work.

---

**Power Quote**

*If Your Sex Life Is Important To You…*
*You Will Find A Way,*
*If Not You Will Find An Excuse.*

---

Good luck finding the time. Most people find all sorts of excuses for why they don't have time for sex. The sex act itself really doesn't take very long, on average it takes about 10 to 16 minutes. But foreplay and afterplay can take a significant amount of time. If you think you don't have time for sex, you probably mean you don't have the time to set a romantic mood or feel sexy. So whether you just want to squeeze in a quickie, or have the time for making love to your MAN, here is a game you can use.

Take two bags, write down the 7 days of the week on 7 pieces of paper, place this in bag 1 and write down on 4 pieces of paper 4x1 hour slots when you both can be free and place in bag 2... *"Remember can be free!"* Now pick one from each bag and you both must do whatever it takes to get that day and time free; like get a baby sitter, leave the kids with friends, and if all else fail... have sex in the car or book a room if you stay with other people.

*Take Notes.*

_____

_____

_____

_____

---

## Power Quote

*Nobody Can Bring You Victory But Yourself*

# <u>Just Between The Two Of You</u>

Create your top six sex values. The words or phrases in the list below maybe your sex values. Not all these values will be important ones, but they are all values. Choose six, putting them in order of importance and tell your MAN why you have chosen them and the he gets to choose his six, putting them in order of importance and must tell you why he picked them.

The words or phrases below have been used with my clients and have lead to some amazing results. These may mean a pain value or a pleasure value, or even both. You can choose whether you want to be in the bedroom, which could be quite exciting, or you can be on the couch talking but you both have to be in the same room for this to work very well and not on the telephone.

I wrote this book for you but it's a book to help both men and women.

| Excitement | Romance | Annoying |
|---|---|---|
| Risk | Depressing | Relaxing |
| Embarrassing | Freedom | Tense |
| Eroticism | Disgusting | Angry |
| Wildness | Animal | Mystery |
| Comfort | Pressurized | Thrilling |
| Boring | Hunger | Sensual |
| Intensity | Unifying | Compassionate |
| Dirty | Friendly | Swallow |
| Intimacy | Ecstatic | Generous |
| Love | Uncontrollable | Urgent |
| Mystical | Sex Toys | Primitive |
| Virginity | Memorable | Satisfaction |
| Silly | Threatening | Emotional |
| Exploitative | Mastery | Powerful |
| Pain | Passionate | Imagination |
| Tiring | Gentle | Condoms |
| Satisfying | Frightening | Foreplay |
| Energetic | Size | Trust |
| Lust | Taste | Scent |
| Underwear | Beauty | Challenge |
| Sexiness | Flirting | Honesty |
| Marriage | Jealousy | Multiple Orgasms |

"The MANual To Amazing Sex"

## You First:

1._____

2._____

3._____

4._____

5._____

6._____

## Your MAN Next:

1._____

2._____

3._____

4._____

5._____

6._____

---

# Power Quote

### *Sharing Is The New Sexy.*

---

# Let The Kama Sutra Games Begin

The Kama Sutra is the bible of sex positions. It was written in India in Sanskrit. Historian's think it first appeared between 400 BCE and 200CE! Originally it wasn't just a sex positions manual but a whole way of life! However, if it's sex positions you're after then you've come to the right place! The Kama Sutra contains very detailed instructions to different sex positions.

Being Indian myself that means my forefathers have made this, and I'm going to give you some fun games to play. The Kama Sutra provides both a way of approaching sex with attention and open mindedness, and a catalog of sexual positions, some quite erotic. Exploring the Kama Sutra will help you find new freedom and playfulness in your lovemaking.
There are a number of translations available in good book stores and online.

---

# Power Quote

*The Most Precious Gift That You Can Give*

*To Your Sex Life, Is The Gift Of...*

*Your Attention.*

---

You will need to get a copy of this book to

play these games.

*Take Notes.*


1. Play Kama Sutra dice. (You need two dice) Best of three

and the winner gets to choose a position.

_____

_____

_____

_____

_____

_____

_____

2. Make up your own Kama Sutra photo album with numbered photos. Pick a number, or close your eyes and point to a page to see what position to achieve.

_____

_____

_____

_____

_____

_____

_____

3. Use a dice and six photos of your favorite Kama Sutra positions numbering them one to six. Roll the dice and spend 4 minutes in the position before rolling the dice again to continue.

_____

_____

_____

_____

_____

_____

_____

4. Buy a pack of Kama Sutra playing card (online or in sex shops). Play "Go Fish." The winner earns sex in their favorite position.

_____

_____

_____

_____

_____

_____

_____

---

## Power Quote

*KamaSutra Is When Fate Fucks You In All Sorts Of Creative Sexual Ways.*

---

# Feedback To Yourself

1. What was my biggest insight whilst I was reading this chapter?

_____

_____

_____

_____

2. What action will I take now after reading this chapter?

_____

_____

_____

_____

3. What support do I need to take this action?

_____

_____

_____

_____

# KIDS GAMES WITH YOUR MAN

Having fun with your MAN may be just what
The Sex Coach ordered! Being playful will get you
connecting in a very fun way. You don't have to do all the
games but you will see, the more you play them the more
open your MAN will be with you.

Adding a bet can be more playful and this will make your
MAN want to play full out to win. And the Winner gets...?
(Make two prizes, one for him and one for you.) Try never
to change the prizes, don't make it too costly for the other
person and remember you love this person.
Now lets have some fun…

---

### Power Quote

*If You Want Amazing Sex, This Must First
Start With You.*

---

*Take Notes.*

1. Play zoo and pretend you're the animal of your choice. Make love as that animal. Be as wild, or sleek, or slippery as you like.

_____

_____

_____

_____

_____

2. Have a three-legged race. Tape or tie one leg each together and try having sex now.

_____

_____

_____

_____

_____

3. Play Spin the Bottle and only foreplay with no kissing.

_____

_____

_____

4. Play "Sexual Truth or Dare" if you have not in the last chapter.

5. Play naked Twister.

6. Play strip-dice. Take turns rolling two dices and the one with the lowest number has to seductively remove a piece of clothing.

_____

_____

_____

_____

_____

7. Play strip poker, but start by taking underwear off first.

_____

_____

_____

_____

_____

---

## Power Quote

*It's Amazing When You Can Act Like A Child And Think There Is Nothing Stopping You.*

---

8. Play naked statues and see who can hold still longer.

_____

_____

_____

_____

_____

9. Stand naked in front of each other. Become mirror images and mime each other's movements.

_____

_____

_____

_____

_____

## Power Quote

*You Are 100% Responsible For Your Sexual Energy.*

*Are You Enjoying This Book?*
Let me know on Twitter.

*My Twitter is: @Cvc4v*

# Feedback To Yourself

1. What was my biggest insight whilst I was reading this chapter?

_____

_____

_____

_____

2. What action will I take now after reading this chapter?

_____

_____

_____

_____

3. What support do I need to take this action?

_____

_____

_____

_____

# DESIGNER SEX WITH YOUR MAN

As the heading says, this is your time to create something new with your MAN and this will make you stand out from all the other women who are just plain boring in the bedroom.

Wondering how you can do this now?

It's by reading this book a few times and working together to see what works for you. Here are some ideas that will help you faster. Enjoy!

*Take Notes.*

---

## Power Quote

***Your Sex Life Will Never Be The Same Again.***

---

1. Design a sexual technique or new sexual position you have not done together before and name this after yourselves.

---

_____

_____

_____

2. Invent a technique, create a story, or organize an erotic evening that will make your MAN reach an orgasm without being touched.

_____

_____

_____

_____

_____

3. Make a list of sexy ideas and whisper them into your MAN's ear. Ask your MAN to rate the ideas on a scale of one to ten.

_____

_____

_____

_____

_____

4. Research sexual techniques from different cultures with your MAN and do some of them.

_____

_____

_____

_____

_____

5. Imagine any part of your MAN's body as a warm peach or juicy MANgo.

Take your time as you devour him all over.

_____

_____

_____

_____

_____

## Power Quote

*I Don't Do Sexy. I Am Sexy.*

# Feedback To Yourself

1. What was my biggest insight whilst I was reading this chapter?

_____

_____

_____

_____

2. What action will I take now after reading this chapter?

_____

_____

_____

_____

3. What support do I need to take this action?

_____

_____

_____

_____

# BODY TALK, TELL US WHAT YOU WANT?

Imagine your various body parts could talk and ask for what they want, say what mood they are in, or express their likes and dislikes. What would they say?

1. If your vagina could talk, how would she say she is feeling right now?

_____

_____

_____

_____

_____

_____

_____

2. If his penis could talk, where would he want to be?

_____

_____

_____

_____

_____

_____

_____

3. If your breasts could talk, what would they request?

_____

_____

_____

_____

_____

4. If your hands could talk, what would they say and what would they want to do?

_____

_____

_____

_____

_____

_____

_____

5. Is there any neglected body parts that would like to ask for attention?

_____

_____

_____

_____

_____

_____

_____

***Want Me To Be Your Coach?***
Feel free to call me.

*My mobile number is: +(44) 778899 5678*

# Feedback To Yourself

1. What was my biggest insight whilst I was reading this chapter?

_____

_____

_____

_____

2. What action will I take now after reading this chapter?

_____

_____

_____

_____

3. What support do I need to take this action?

_____

_____

_____

_____

## COCK SUCKING TECHNIQUES
### *(WARNING, NOT FOR WEAK THROATS)*

Your MAN's cock is truly the key to his mind. Unlike your sexuality, which encompasses your entire body and is as emotional as it is physical, your MAN's sexuality is centered in this one physical organ. Loving it, touching it, placing it in your mouth and other body parts will not only please him physically it will also create a deep emotional bond between the two of you. Your MAN will always say "YES" if you say you need a volunteer to do this.

---

## Power Quote

### *Always Remember This Ladies,*
### *Blowjobs Are Like Flowers To Your MAN.*

---

When doing this, I would recommend a shower or bath beforehand, as this will make both of you feel good. After a few weeks ask him if you can wash his cock for him with some soap and water first. Watch his eyes and how his body moves while washing his cock.

## Deep Throat

First and foremost ladies you've got to learn how to deep throat. I know that when you are first starting out it can be kind of intimidating, especially if you're with someone of a large stature. But with practice you can learn to take pretty much the entire shaft of most men all the way into your throat. The way to learn this is by starting out small. I don't mean cock size, I mean by inching your way down the penis, lower and lower, until eventually you can take in the whole thing. This is not going to happen in one day, you have to train your gag reflex not to respond, and for those of you girls that are bulimic ignore deep throating because you have already trained your gag reflex to do the opposite, so good luck trying to undo this. Also when you have the entire cock in your mouth it doesn't have to stay there for eternity, go back up to the top and play around until you are ready to go back down again. You just have to experiment until you get your own style.

## <u>Suck Everything</u>

Many women have a fear of balls. Why? I do not know. There is a lot of feeling in the testicular area for men, so if you don't want to touch them there they are not going to be happy with you. If you have a paranoia of smell or dirt have your MAN take a shower before you do this. Better still, shower together as this can work wonders for *you* if you are uncomfortable during this. Once you know that he is good and clean lick him all over and definitely get the balls in your mouth, one at a time, but do it gently. Your MAN is oversensitive in this area so you must have good communication to prevent any unwanted stimulation. Also lick him right underneath his balls, the G-spot is right on the other side of this spot. If you gently push your tongue onto this area it will create subtle stimulation on his G-spot.

Some people are into this and some are not. Depending on your MAN, you can go to the asshole. This is not something you should do without discussing first, especially if you are new to this person. And if they like this, try it out? Showering first is a great idea here.

## **Timing**

I know this title sounds a bit boring, but it can really make or break your blowjob. Now I know that most of you have masturbated, so think about how it feels when you just get off really fast, like you have an event to go to and you just pull one off quick in the public bathroom before an interview. Now think about when you are at home alone on a Sunday and you see something raunchy or sexy on TV and then you play around with yourself for a while out of habit until you get down to the dirty. You don't let yourself cum right away, you arouse yourself almost to climax, then simmer down and do that a few times until you explode. That's how cock sucking works. You can't just get it in your mouth and hit it really hard, like having your face fucked in the first four seconds. You have to tease it for a while. Caress it, use your hands, your arms, your body, and slowly ever so slowly, stretch out your tongue and give it a little lick. Then sit back and look at his cock, wait a second, then do it again. At this point he is aching for you so badly to shove the whole engorged thing into your mouth, he is going to feel like it's about to explode. Basically what you are do now is taunting him, and don't give him what he wants until *you* decide it's time, and the longer that you can hold out from giving in to fully fledged face fuck the better his orgasm is going to be.

## **Hand And Mouth Co-Ordination**

This is another one of those things that comes with practice. Being able to work with the motion of both of your hands and your mouth takes skill. First lets just talk about the hands. You have two for a reason. My one client preferred using one for the balls and the other to work on the shaft. The hand that is used for the balls should be very gentle and should never violently grab them or you may lose your chance of ever trying this again. She would gently stroke them flipping her hand upside down using both the top and bottom part of her hand. Once she had done that for a while she would cup them but never just let them be still, the hand must always be subtly moving for constant stimulation. The other hand must be working with the up and down movement of the head. The timing has to be right on this as well because if you are constantly crashing into your face with your hand that won't work. Sometimes she would come up off of the shaft with her head and just let her hand take over for a little while. This gives your mouth a break, especially if you've been deep throating, and allows for the hand to perform the type of movement that your head cannot, like moving up and down rapidly.

If you can get these three things to work together, your MAN will think the world of you. *Trust me!*

## To Spit Or To Swallow?

This is always a hot topic. There are always the few loud people in the crowd who try to convince all the girls to swallow. But really most guys just want to be able to cum in your mouth. This does not mean that you need to swallow. If you like the taste of cum and it does not gross you out, by all means swallow, but if that's not the case just spit it out. It's after the act and generally guys don't care about that.

Just make sure that you leave his cock in your mouth long enough for him to be able to finish cumming, leaving before he is done ejaculating would be upsetting for sure.

---

**Power Quote**

*Spitters Are Quitters.*

---

Here is something I found out while writing this book. Be open to it, as it may help you more than you think. Evidence exists of ancient Indian rituals where women would spread semen on their faces, breasts and hair. Biochemists have found some value in the exercise as semen contains plenty of vitamin C, calcium, proteins and other nutrients, and has antibiotic qualities. It has an astringent effect when spread on the face and leaves it feeling smooth and clean afterwards. This ritual helps a woman recreate her youth and absorb male energy, which is vital for her masculine/feminine balance.

*Take Notes.*

_____

_____

_____

_____

_____

_____

_____

# Feedback To Yourself

## 1. What was my biggest insight whilst I was reading this chapter?

_____

_____

_____

_____

## 2. What action will I take now after reading this chapter?

_____

_____

_____

## 3. What support do I need to take this action?

_____

_____

_____

_____

# GREAT SEX FOODS TO EAT WITH YOUR MAN

In my search to see what works well to get a better enjoyment with your MAN, I did hours of research. I found these foods to be helpful and amazing for you and your MAN.

*Figs* - Ancient Greeks indulged in orgies once the fig harvest was in. They are not only packed with vitamins, but when sliced in half, the ripe, pink flesh is suggestive of the vagina.

*Chocolate* - No one can dispute the aphrodisiac qualities that chocolate contains, being rich in energising chemicals and the darker the better. It also contains phenylethylamine and anandamide, which can give a euphoric effect, the two compounds that cause the body to release the same feel-good endorphins triggered by sex and physical exertion. Cocoa also contains methylxanthines, which make skin sensitive to every touch.

***Almonds*** - Contains zinc, selenium, and vitamin E, which are vitamins and minerals that seem to be important for sexual health and reproduction. Selenium can help with infertility issues and, with vitamin E, may help heart health. Zinc is a mineral that helps produce men's sex hormones and can boost libido. Blood flow is important for your sex organs, so choose good fats, such as the omega-3 fatty acids found in almonds.

***Ginger, Garlic and Onions*** - To really get your juices flowing, pile on the garlic, leeks, onions, scallions and chives. Known as alliums, these powerful vegetables will give you the stamina that pharmaceuticals can only promise. Containing chemical compounds that stimulate blood flow to the genital area, these vegetables cause intense feelings of arousal, resulting in a strong, enduring sex. Breath won't be an issue...and with any luck, you'll be so busy, who'll care?

*Artichokes* - Ancient Romans believed that eating artichokes were not only an aphrodisiac, but would result in everlasting life. They were wrong on the "living forever" part, but these can result in better sex.

*Avocados* - Rich in vitamin E, which has antioxidant properties, potassium, and vitamin B6, which may prevent or delay heart disease and promote better blood flow. They're also a good source of heart-healthy monounsaturated fats. Anything that helps your heart and circulation can also be critical for a healthy sex life. Men with heart disease are twice as likely to have erectile dysfunction because both conditions can result from artery damage.

*Strawberries* - Good circulation is thought to be crucial for sexual functioning in both men and women and strawberries are rich in antioxidants that benefit your heart and arteries. What's more they're rich in vitamin C, which along with antioxidants has been linked to higher sperm count in men. Try dipping the berries in dark chocolate which contains methylxanthines that may activate the libido.

***Watermelon -*** This popular summer fruit is low in calories but also high in potentially libido-boosting phytonutrients. New research suggests that the lycopene, citrulline and beta-carotene found in watermelon may help relax blood vessels and provide a natural enhancement for revving up your sex drive.

***Sunflower, Pumpkin & Sesame Seeds -*** Zinc is thought to be good for sexual health, it can help testosterone and sperm production in men, and the number one source is oysters. But really, how often do you eat oysters? Now new studies show they are beneficial for women too.

***Blueberries -*** Forget Viagra. Mother Nature's original blue potency capsules may do even more for you.

Blueberries are high in soluble fibre, which helps remove excess cholesterol from the blood before it gets absorbed and deposited on artery walls. Blueberries also relax blood vessels and improve blood flow.

*For maximum potency and performance, eat a serving of blueberries at least three or four times a week.*

Studies also show this sweetens your MAN's sperm.

*Take Notes.*

_____

_____

_____

_____

_____

_____

_____

---

## Power Quote

***It's Not A Diet, It's Called Eating Sexily.***

---

# Feedback To Yourself

1. What was my biggest insight whilst I was reading this chapter?

_____

_____

_____

_____

2. What action will I take now after reading this chapter?

_____

_____

_____

3. What support do I need to take this action?

_____

_____

_____

_____

## UNDERSTANDING HIS FANTASIES

To be fair, I was not going to put this chapter into the book, but got lots of feedback from my female clients and friends telling me how great it would be to read how men fantasize. Sorry guys, but this may work to your advantage moving forward. If there is one thing your boyfriend or husband fantasizes about, it's this.

---

### Fair Warning:

*You might not want to hear or read this…*
*If you want to know? Read on.*

---

The one thing all men fantasize about is other women. No matter how much we love you, no matter how beautiful you are, no matter how great you are in bed. We will fantasize about other women.

We will fantasize about our ex, the girl in high school we wish we'd have asked out, our average-looking co-worker, the famous actress in the movie or the girl at the supermarket. Basically, we'll probably fantasize about every attractive woman we've ever seen that we can remember.

Before you get insecure it's important to understand that fantasies are exactly that "just fantasies". Even if we would never even consider cheating on you, we will still fantasize about other women. This does not mean we seriously want to have sex with other women, we just like playing with the idea. Your MAN will probably hate me for telling you this now, but it's the truth. Here are some that I found out myself and by working with my male clients.

---

### Power Quote

*We Fantasize About Other Women.*
*We Can't Help It. We Just Do!!*

---

To understand your MAN better, ask this question: "Will I do any of the following fantasies?

*Take Notes.*

## **<u>Sexy Outfits</u>**

Nurse costumes, schoolgirl outfits, police outfits or airhostess's suits. They're just a few of the many outfits men fantasize about women wearing. While men usually aren't quite as interested in high fashion as women, the right set of clothes will turn many on. You can know this by just asking him and he will be glad to tell you, and don't be afraid to ask because he would love it if you did.

Have you done this or are you willing to do this?

_____

_____

_____

_____

_____

_____

_____

_____

## Love Triangle

Love triangle can refer to having a threesome or a three-way romantic relationship. Though threesome is most commonly applied to a casual sexual activity involving sexual activity among three people.

A threesome is a common sexual fantasy. Yes it's true, the most popular fantasy among men involves having sex with multiple women at the same time. Virtually every straight man will fantasize about it several, or more likely, numerous times in his life. And even if it usually doesn't work out quite as well as you'd hope in real life as a fantasy it is virtually unbeatable.

_____

_____

_____

_____

_____

_____

## <u>See What We Are Doing</u>

The combination of being taboo and involving others is what makes this fantasy a turn-on for quite a few men. Forbidden fruit is always attractive, especially when it comes to sex. When the chance of showing off one's sexual prowess to the world is added to that, it becomes an irresistible fantasy for many. Have you ever tried - Leaving the blinds open for all to see? or having a party in someone else's house and somebody walks in while you are having sex and you don't stop.

Are there any ideas cumming to you now?

_____

_____

_____

_____

_____

_____

_____

# Age Differences Big Or Small

Sometimes it's a simple matter of taste, sometimes a matter of wanting what you don't have and sometimes a matter of nostalgia. It is very common to try this once or even more in one's lifetime. Either way, men often fantasize about women with ages vastly different from their own. Eighteen year old men fantasize about women in their forties, fifty-four year old men fantasize about eighteen year old women, and so on.

Ask yourself this question: " Would I do some one younger or older than me with a 20 year age difference?"

_____

_____

_____

_____

_____

_____

_____

## <u>Going Down South</u>

When it comes to sex acts, one of the most popular that men fantasize about is performing oral sex on women. Both the thought of pleasuring a woman, as well as stimulating senses like taste and scent, make this fantasy incredibly arousing for many men.

Having been with a lot of women myself, most women I know don't like it! Women love giving it because they feel they are in charge. If not it's because of a past experience. Please tell your MAN if you like or want this.

_____

_____

_____

_____

_____

_____

_____

## <u>The Change Of Scenery</u>

"Location, location, location" might be the motto to real estate agents, but for many men it's also a main feature of their fantasies. Whether it's a beach at night, on the hood of his car, in a sunny park in summer or the kitchen, sex in specific places is one of the most exciting fantasies for many men.

Name a few places you want to be with your MAN?

_____

_____

_____

_____

_____

_____

_____

_____

_____

_____

# Watching Porn

It's often said that we men are visual creatures and this fantasy definitely confirms that. Watching a woman masturbate, or watching a couple having sex, are among your MAN's favorite fantasies.

This is not surprising, considering the popularity of porn. Ask your MAN to watch porn with you.

Most women don't like to watch because they feel their body may not be as hot as the ones they see in porn.

_____

_____

_____

_____

_____

_____

_____

_____

# **Giving Up Control**

In a society where men are often expected to take initiative, it shouldn't come as a shock to you that many of them fantasize about doing the exact opposite and completely giving up control to a woman. Fantasies involving this range from simply being told what to do in the bedroom, to being tied up and ravished by you. Do you want to be in charge? If your answer "Yes" then have turns in the bedroom and ask a lot of questions.

_____

_____

_____

_____

_____

_____

_____

_____

# Try This Out

Finally, before you go out and fight with your MAN, a word of wisdom.

Even if these are popular fantasies, every man is different.

The best way to find out what your MAN fantasizes about is by simply *asking him* and not being a mind reader or by reading any articles on the Internet.

Please always keep this in your mind. Some fantasies are best left unfulfilled.

---

**Power Quote**

*If You Never Ask, You Will Never Know?*

*You Will Always Know If It's Right For You.*

---

## Your Four Fantasies:

1. _____

_____

_____

2. _____

_____

_____

3. _____

_____

_____

4. _____

_____

_____

---

## Power Quote

*Trust Is The Best Lubrication For Amazing Sex.*

---

## Your MAN's Four Fantasies:

1. _____

_____

_____

2. _____

_____

_____

3. _____

_____

_____

4. _____

_____

_____

### *Enjoying This Book?*
Email me a photo of you with the book.

*My email address is: ShareWithMe@c4v.co.uk*

# Feedback To Yourself

1. What was my biggest insight whilst I was reading this chapter?

_____

_____

_____

_____

2. What action will I take now after reading this chapter?

_____

_____

_____

3. What support do I need to take this action?

_____

_____

_____

_____

# TO ROLE PLAY OR NOT TO ROLE PLAY

Remember how you used to spend endless hours playing when you were a child? How you used your imagination to create all sorts of alternatives realities? It's just when you grow up, you find yourself using your imaginations less and being more inhibited than you used to be.

This can be fun to escape for a while. To be adventurous or to be someone else and at the same time it pushes your sexual boundaries.

Here are some scenarios I have cum up with for you to play with. Have fun with them.

*Take Notes.*

---

### Power Quote

*Don't See The Change,*

*Be The Change In The Bedroom.*

---

# The Sex Coach and Client

Toss a coin to see who takes the role of the Client.

Scenario: The Sex Coach has to go somewhere private to be able to answer the call of the Client. The Client rings up the Sex Coach and pretends to ask them for suggestions on how to please their partner (which is you). The Sex Coach goes into great detail describing a few ways to please their partner (what you like).
For this to work very well, the Client must write down whatever is said and ask any questions if confused.

_____

_____

_____

_____

_____

_____

_____

## Master/Mistress and Slave

Toss a coin to see who takes the role of Slave.

Scenario: Once the roles have been established, the Slave has to carry out every action required of them without question. For this to work very well you must pick only one: (use a timer or have a secret word) so if it gets too much for the Slave they can stop. You must also change roles to give both a chance to be the Slave to be fair.

_____

_____

_____

_____

_____

_____

_____

_____

# Barman/Barmaid and Customer

Toss a coin to see who is the Barman or Barmaid.

Scenario: The Customer orders a drink from the bar but has no money and has already drunk the drink. What does the Barman/Barmaid being single do as the customer is their type, and it's been a while since they had some sex? Offer to pay for the drink for XXX with you in return or can you come up with some other offers?

_____

_____

_____

_____

_____

_____

_____

_____

_____

# Phone Sex Hotline and Caller

Toss a coin to see who takes the role of the Caller.

Scenario: The Caller has to go somewhere private to be able to call of the Phone Sex Hotline. The Caller rings up the Sex Hotline and asks to be turned on with a sexy story. The Sex Hotline person goes into great detail describing a story how they are going to make the Caller cum. For this to work very well, the Caller needs to tell them a sexual fantasy they want to hear.

_____

_____

_____

_____

_____

_____

_____

## Head Master/Mistress and Student

Toss a coin to see who takes the role as the Head Master/Mistress.

Scenario 1: A disciplinarian head mistress punishes the naughty schoolboy for persistently bad behaviour. Here she will make you write down and repeat all those dirty (sexually related) sentences you wrote down and read them back to her. There's a chance she could well spank you - you'd better be MAN enough to take it.

Scenario 2: A mini skirted schoolgirl refusing to conform to school dress policy is sent to her head master that proceeds to lay her over his knee and dish out a pleasurable form of discipline.

_____

_____

_____

_____

# Cop and Robber

Toss a coin to see who takes the role as the Robber.

Scenario 1: You've been caught red-handed trying to break into the house (swag bag and mask optional) by a very sexy cop of the law (minimal police uniform compulsory). To prevent you escaping they handcuff you to a chair or bed before blindfolding you and beginning with their interrogation. You then proceed to taunt and tease the Robber, whispering what you going do to them, where you will touch next, and how the Robber is unable to do anything about it.

Scenario 2: Change your role to an Undercover Cop (The Robber) after they have had their fun with you and now they are the Dirty Cop in trouble with you.

_____

_____

_____

# Feedback To Yourself

1. What was my biggest insight whilst I was reading this chapter?

_____

_____

_____

_____

2. What action will I take now after reading this chapter?

_____

_____

_____

_____

3. What support do I need to take this action?

_____

_____

_____

_____

"The MANual To Amazing Sex"

# *Here Is A Small Advertisement*

You don't have to read it. As there's a spare white page here I thought it would be a good time to shamelessly advertise some of the things I do, just in case they are of interest to you.

I offer training in various different forms:

Intervention With The Sex Coach™
The Mind Fuck Bootcamp™ (3 Days)
Dinner With The Sex Coach™
CSI - Cv's Sex Investigation™ (TV/Radio Show)
Hen Night With The Sex Coach™
Cum Sex With Me™ (Holidays)
Love Sex Angel™
(Online Sex Programs… Cumming Soon)

Now and again I talk at conferences and corporate events, either on subjects related to this book or on "strange things" such as using your mind to achieve impossible results. For more details, call me.
Mobile: +(44) 778899 5678

I love travelling around the world and I'm happy to work/talk anywhere (work visa permitting). I am terribly expensive, as you'd expect, but try to focus on the quality and value, *not* the price.

# Q&A TIME

Read and answer Yes or No? And Why?

There are no wrong answers over here. The point of this Q&A is to discuss your sexual views with your MAN's sexual views. Writing your answers down will make it more real and gives more understanding to you both.

---

## Power Quote

### *You Can Only Really Lie To One Person, Yourself.*

---

## Time For You

1. Seeing your naked body doesn't do anything for me.

_____

_____

_____

_____

_____

2. Having sex without love doesn't give me pleasure.

_____

_____

_____

_____

_____

3. It takes a lot to excite me sexually.

_____

_____

_____

_____

4. I think about sex several times a day.

_____

_____

_____

_____

_____

## 5. The idea of an orgy turns me on.

_____

_____

_____

_____

_____

## 6. I sometimes have a guilty conscience after sex.

_____

_____

_____

_____

## 7. I've had some bad sexual experiences.

_____

_____

_____

_____

## 8. Watching porn turns me on.

_____

_____

_____

_____

_____

## **Time For Your MAN**

### 1. Seeing your naked body doesn't do anything for me.

_____

_____

_____

_____

### 2. Having sex without love doesn't give me pleasure.

_____

_____

_____

_____

3. It takes a lot to excite me sexually.

4. I think about sex several times a day.

5. The idea of an orgy turns me on.

6. I sometimes have a guilty conscience after sex.

_____

_____

_____

_____

_____

7. I've had some bad sexual experiences.

_____

_____

_____

_____

8. Watching porn turns me on.

_____

_____

_____

_____

# Feedback To Yourself

1. What was my biggest insight whilst I was reading this chapter?

_____

_____

_____

_____

2. What action will I take now after reading this chapter?

_____

_____

_____

_____

3. What support do I need to take this action?

_____

_____

_____

_____

# LETS TALK ABOUT SEX AND MEET

# FOR COFFEE™

## *"The Art Of Online Dating"*

This is a Limited Edition Bonus just for you now.

The processes you are about to read are from my next book

coming out next year.

Email me to if you want to learn how to get a positive

sexual energy in only two questions.

These processes that I have created have helped lots of my

clients and may help you too.

*Read the testimonial on the back cover to*

*see what I mean.*

---

**Trust The Process:**

*Please Finish Each Page Before Moving On.*

---

## SOUL MATE FINDER™

I want you to say: "Yes That's Me" if you skipped all the chapters and came straight to this game. Most people would say, "I am looking for my soul mate." Write down six things you will be offering to your soul mate within the next ten minutes.

1._____

2._____

3._____

4._____

5._____

6._____

---

## Read This:

*Please Finish This First Page Before Moving On.*

---

Now write down six things you want from him (single)

or he is offering to you (in a relationship)

Again you will only have ten minutes to do this.

1._____

2._____

3._____

4._____

5._____

6._____

---

## **Read This:**

*Please Finish This Page Before Moving On.*

---

Now you are wondering, 'How does this work?

Here is "The Mind Fuck".

If three or more don't match then you may need look at

what you are offering, or maybe he is just not

your soul mate.

Soul mates normally think alike. Yes?

Now one is different because we all don't have the same

fingerprints and the other one is that, we are all different in

some way or the other.

You may not like or understand this finder but it does

works. If you have a better way how to find your

Soul Mate? Please let me know.

---

## Power Quote

*You Will Find Your Soul Mate,*
*Just Like How The Stars Come Out…*
*And You Two Will Shine.*

---

# HOW TO GET YOUR MR RIGHT?™

That's easy. He's already in your head. This easy exercise will hone in the qualities or the features you want in your MAN. For this game, fill in 1-10 below with the things you want from your MAN, for example tall, short, muscular, skinny, intelligent, funny, honest, trustworthy, and those are examples. You can use these or make up your own. You will have ten minutes only to do this.

1._____

2._____

3._____

4._____

5._____

6._____

7._____

8._____

9._____

10._____

"The MANual To Amazing Sex"

After writing your ten down, I want you to choose four that you really don't want with a (-) next to them. You have four minutes to do this. I trust you that you can time yourself again. After finishing that write it down here and read aloud the four that you have put the (-) next to.

1._____

2._____

3._____

4._____

---

## Read This:

*Please Finish This Page Before Moving On.*

---

Now I want you to choose a further four that you really don't want with a (*) next to them. You have four minutes again. I trust you that you can time yourself. After finishing that write it down here and read aloud the four that you have put the (*) next to.

1._____

2._____

3._____

4._____

---

## Read This:

*Please Finish This Page Before Moving On.*

---

From the eight that you have chosen, I want you to choose two that you really don't want with a (x) next to them. You have two minutes to do that. I trust you that you can time yourself. After finishing that write it down here and read aloud the two that you have put the (x) next to.

1._____

2._____

---

## **Read This:**

*Please Finish This Page Before Moving On.*

---

Okay! Now answer this question next. "Is this *your* list?"

Yes or No? If your answer is "*Yes*"?

Proceed to the next question.

Are you okay with the two that you really don't want?

Here is another "Mind Fuck".

*These are the only two things that you must look for in your next MAN and only those two things.*

You see, you are looking for so many things in a MAN at any given time that your mind gets confused.

This is a simple way I created to de-clutter your mind because this is your list and it's all your choices. *Yes?*

From "*the worst to the best*" because what you think you don't really want, are still the qualities you are looking for in your MAN.


### *Want Positive Sexual Energy?*
Email me and ask me for the two questions?

*My email is: ShareWithMe@c4v.co.uk*

# Feedback To Yourself

1. What was my biggest insight whilst I was reading the bonuses?

_____

_____

_____

_____

2. What action will I take now after reading the bonuses?

_____

_____

_____

3. What support do I need to take this action?

_____

_____

_____

_____

# CURTAIN CLOSE…

This brings to a close
The Secrets Your Mama Didn't Tell You About Men™
I hope that you found this book interesting and worthwhile.

If you want to get in touch, or work with me…
Call me to book a consultation, a half day Intensive Sex
Coaching Session or if you feel adventurous book me for a
weekend away on your chosen holiday destination:
+(44) 778899 5678

May I once again thank all of those who helped
to produce this book and most of all
I would like to thank YOU for reading my book.

Cv Pillay
01 June 2014, London

# PASS IT ON!

Did you like this book? If you did, I ask to you to tell other people about it.

I bet you have an email list of friends and contacts. Why not send round a 'group email' about this book and its contents.

Post messages about it on Facebook, Twitter, BBM or on any Social Media that you use.

Mark your copy so people know it's your property, and leave it in any common area where you work, play, or meet other people. It could be a quite a conversation starter.

Got friends or contacts in the media? Tell them about the book. They might get a good story, article or feature out of it! (I am easily contacted via Skype.) Do you contribute to a magazine? Why not write a short review of the book, and mention how to order a copy?

# THANK YOU!

Cv Pillay

www.c4v.co.uk

Mobile: +(44) 778899 5678

Email: ShareWithMe@c4v.co.uk

Facebook: Coaching 4 Victory Quotes

Facebook: Cv.co.uk

Twitter: @Cvc4v

Skype: c4v.ltd

---

## Power Quote

*Live Today Like It's Your Last Day…*

*But Pay Me First And Use A Condom,*

*Just In Case It's Not!*

---

# NOTES

"The MANual To Amazing Sex"

# NOTES

_____

_____

_____

_____

_____

_____

_____

_____

_____

_____

_____

_____

_____

_____

_____

_____